Echoes
from the
Higher
Ground

Table of Contents

Dedication i

Foreword iii

Preface v

Introduction vii

Chapter I The Heart Behind the Law
— Anger, Lust, and Divorce 1

Chapter II Let Your Yes Be Yes
— Truth in Speech 7

Chapter III Turning the Other Cheek
— The Fire of Mercy 11

Chapter IV Love Your Enemies
— The Perfection of the Father 15

Chapter V The Secret Life
— Giving Without Applause 19

Chapter VI When You Pray
— Enter the Secret Place 23

Chapter VII Hallowed Be Thy Name
— Unlocking the Lord's Prayer 27

Chapter VIII Thy Kingdom Come
— The Surrender of Sovereignty 31

Chapter IX Daily Bread
— Trusting God for Today 35

Chapter X Forgive Us
— The Link Between Mercy and Freedom 39

Chapter XI Lead Us Not Into Temptation
— The Prayer for Guidance and Strength 43

Chapter XII For Thine Is the Kingdom
— Living in the Power of the Amen 47

Conclusion 53

Acknowledgments 55

About the Author 57

Back Cover Blurb 59

Dedication

To the quiet ones — those who pray in secret, love without applause, and walk the narrow way when no one else is watching.

You are the true children of the mountain.

And to my beloved wife, Feebe, whose strength is silent, whose faith is loud, and whose love echoes deeper than words.

You help me hear Him—still.

Foreword

There are sermons, and then there is The Sermon.

Spoken from a Galilean mountaintop by a wandering rabbi with no army, no throne, and no wealth — this message altered the course of history, not through conquest, but through conviction.

In a world that glorified power, Jesus praised meekness.

In an age ruled by empires, He declared the blessedness of the poor in spirit.

And in a culture bent on vengeance, He introduced the scandal of forgiveness.

It wasn't just a message — it was a mirror to every soul, a manifesto for Heaven's Kingdom, and a call to a life so upside-down it could only be right-side up in eternity.

Preface

This book was born on my knees.
Not in theory, but in tears.
Not in study, but in surrender.

I didn't set out to write a sequel.

I set out to listen — to the same Mountain Voice that first whispered to fishermen, tax collectors, and the brokenhearted.

The Mountain Still Speaks, Volume I traced the opening lines of Christ's most dangerous sermon.

It carried us through the Beatitudes and into the heart of the Kingdom.
But I couldn't stop there — because he didn't stop there.
He kept going.
Deeper.
Sharper.
Higher.

What began as blessings became commands.
What began as comfort became confrontation.
And what began as poetry became prophecy—about what His disciples must become.

This volume picks up that fire.
It begins with "You have heard…" and ends with "Thine is the Kingdom."

In between, we find a path not of applause, but of obedience.

These pages are not meant to be read quickly.

They are meant to be entered — like a narrow gate, like a sacred fast, like a secret room where only your soul and the Spirit can meet.

I wrote this for the ones still hungry.

The ones who want more than inspiration.

The ones ready to be ruined for anything less than the Kingdom of Heaven.

If that's you, then welcome.

Let us climb again.

And listen.

Still, He speaks.

— **D.B.C.**

Introduction

Still He Speaks

The mountain did not fall silent when the Beatitudes ended.
It only began to burn deeper.

The first volume of this message—Christ's opening blessings, His call to salt and light, and his bold declaration of fulfillment—was the Kingdom's welcome. But what follows is the Kingdom's cost.

Now the mountain speaks again.
And the fire intensifies.

This second ascent climbs into the radical teachings that have split empires, broken the pride of the religious, and remade lives for two thousand years. Here Jesus redefines righteousness, reclaims the Torah, and speaks with an authority so pure it silences every other voice.

These are not sayings for the faint of heart.
They are for the ones who still climb.
We begin where He begins:
"You have heard… but I say unto you."

This is not a new law—it is the eternal law made flesh.
Not the abolishing of holiness, but the reformation of the human heart.

So come again.
Bring your whole self—unarmed, unhidden.

The mountain still speaks.
Still.
Now.
Again.
And these pages are your invitation to listen.

— Damiano B. Centola

This book, Volume II of The Mountain Still Speaks, doesn't attempt to tame that sermon.

Instead, it lets it echo—freely, fiercely, and faithfully—through the soul of a modern listener.

Each chapter is a step deeper into the narrow way.
Each reflection is a reminder that Jesus wasn't offering advice — He was issuing an invitation to transformation.
As you read these pages, you won't just learn what the Sermon meant.
You will feel what it still means.
Because His voice hasn't faded.
His truth hasn't softened.
And His mountain still speaks.

May you have ears to hear, courage to follow, and grace to become what this Sermon calls you to be:
Light in the dark, salt in the decay, fire in a cold world.

Still He speaks.
Will you listen?

— D.B.C.

Chapter I
The Heart Behind the Law — Anger, Lust, and Divorce

> *"Ye have heard that it was said by them of old time, Thou shalt not kill... But I say unto you, That whosoever is angry with his brother without a cause shall be in danger of the judgment... Ye have heard that it was said... Thou shalt not commit adultery: But I say unto you, That whosoever looketh on a woman to lust after her hath committed adultery with her already in his heart... It hath been said, Whosoever shall put away his wife, let him give her a writing of divorcement: But I say unto you..."*
>
> —*Matthew 5:21–32, KJV*

The King now descends deeper—not into the crowds, but into the chambers of the heart.

He does not attack murderers. He confronts bitterness.

He does not denounce adulterers. He exposes desire.

He does not shame the divorced. He reveals the hardness behind the fracture.

This is no longer about law. It is about motive.

No longer about what hands do, but what hearts hide.

Jesus peels back the surface—and the mountain becomes a mirror.

1. Anger — The Seed of Murder

"Thou shalt not kill."

But I say unto you… anger is already dangerous.

Anger is not new.

Cain felt it before his hands reached for Abel.

It is the whisper that precedes every scream, every war, every broken brotherhood.

Jesus is not saying that all anger is sin.

Even the Scriptures say, *"Be ye angry, and sin not." (Eph. 4:26)*

But this is anger without cause.

Anger that festers.

Anger that assigns worthlessness to a brother.

Anger that speaks in dismissive labels:

"Raca" (fool), "worthless," "nothing."

This kind of anger is the murder of the soul, even if no blood is shed.

Jesus places such anger in the courtroom of divine judgment.

Why?

Because the Kingdom of God is built on reconciliation, not rivalry.

And He offers a way out:

"First be reconciled to thy brother…"

Before you offer God your worship, offer your brother your apology.

Jesus is not lowering the bar. He's lifting the soul.

2. Lust — The Fire Behind Adultery

"Thou shalt not commit adultery."

But I say unto you… whoever looks to lust has already fallen.

The scribes dealt with the act.

Jesus deals with the appetite.

Lust is not about noticing beauty.

It is about reducing a soul to an object.

It is the theft of dignity under the disguise of a glance.

Jesus makes no room for compromise.

He uses surgical language:

> "If thy right eye offend thee, pluck it out…
>
> If thy right hand offend thee, cut it off…"

He does not mean literal mutilation.

He means ruthless separation.

What you feed, lives.

What you tolerate, grows.

What you entertain in secret will shout in time.

Jesus is calling His people to a new way of seeing—

Where desire is no longer master.

Where eyes become sanctified windows to Heaven.

This is not repression.

This is freedom.

3. Divorce — The Broken Covenant

> "Whosoever shall put away his wife, let him give her a writing of divorcement."

But I say unto you… except it be for fornication, you cause her to commit adultery.

In the days of Jesus, men could discard their wives for nearly anything:

A ruined meal.

A bad mood.

A fading beauty.

It was legal—but it was not holy.

Jesus points back to Genesis, not Deuteronomy.

Back to covenant, not convenience.

Back to the one flesh mystery, not the loopholes in the law.

"What therefore God hath joined together, let not man put asunder."
(Matthew 19:6)

Jesus is not shaming the divorced.

He is shaming the hardness of heart that treated covenant like a contract.

He is grieving the flippancy with which sacred vows were broken.

He does not ignore infidelity—He permits separation in cases of unfaithfulness.

But He calls all people to tremble before the altar of commitment.

Marriage is not disposable.

It is divine.

The Heart: Heaven's Battlefield

These three topics—anger, lust, and divorce—may seem separate.

But they are linked by a single thread:

the war inside the human heart.

Jesus is not changing the law.

He is reclaiming its heart.

- From murder to malice.
- From adultery to appetite.
- From divorce to disregard.

He is forming a people whose righteousness is not performative, but penetrating.

Whose holiness is not memorized, but embodied.

The Pharisees sought compliance.

Jesus seeks transformation.

Grace for the Battle Within

This chapter is not a burden.

It is an invitation to freedom.

Jesus never exposes without offering healing.

He does not tear down without building something eternal in its place.

If anger has lodged in your chest—He offers reconciliation.

If lust has dulled your vision—He offers purity.

If covenant has been broken—He offers redemption and wisdom.

He is not only the Judge.

He is the Healer of motives.

Let the Mountain Speak

The mountain still speaks—and now it speaks directly to the unseen war within us.

Not to shame, but to liberate.

Not to accuse, but to transform.

Let the Spirit search your heart.

Let Jesus become not only your Savior, but the Lord of your motives.

The Kingdom is not built by those who look holy.

It is built by those whose hearts have been set on fire by the presence of the King.

So look inward.

Lay it bare.

And let the mercy of God shape you from the inside out.

Chapter II
Let Your Yes Be Yes — Truth in Speech

"Again, ye have heard that it hath been said by them of old time, Thou shalt not forswear thyself, but shalt perform unto the Lord thine oaths:
But I say unto you, Swear not at all... But let your communication be, Yea, yea; Nay, nay: for whatsoever is more than these cometh of evil."
—Matthew 5:33–37, KJV

A mountain doesn't need to scream to shake the ground beneath you.
Sometimes it only whispers — "Let your yes be yes."
And yet in this gentle phrase, Jesus unveils a deep fracture in human character: the failure to tell the truth.
This isn't about courtroom swearing.
This is about everyday speech — where exaggeration, manipulation, and half-truths erode the soul's integrity.

It's about truthfulness without spectacle.

Honesty without oath.

And a life so rooted in the Kingdom that it doesn't need extra words to make its promises believable.

The World of Oaths

In Jesus' day, people swore constantly.

To Heaven.

To Jerusalem.

To the gold of the Temple.

To the hairs on their head.

Each oath was a way of saying, "I really mean it this time."

It was a culture where truth was negotiable — and the more you swore, the less people trusted your word.

But Jesus calls His people to live above this broken system.

"Swear not at all…"

Why?

Because truth should not require theatrics.

It should inhabit your every word.

The Simplicity of the Kingdom

"Let your yea be yea; and your nay, nay…"

This is not legalism.

It is liberation from linguistic manipulation.

Jesus invites you to become a person whose speech reflects your soul.

Whose words are not colored with flattery, manipulation, or dramatics.

Whose promises do not need spiritual sounding clauses to prove credibility.

It's not about never making promises.

It's about being the kind of person whose life is the promise.

In the Kingdom of God, truth is not a performance — it is a person.

The Root of Deception

"Whatsoever is more than these cometh of evil…"

This is not a light statement.

Jesus is saying that the need to manipulate language reveals a spiritual fracture — a lack of trust, a need for control, a fear of being known.

Where deception begins, the enemy lurks.

Where truth reigns, the Kingdom advances.

The Devil is called "the father of lies."

But Jesus is called "the Truth."

To speak truth is not merely moral.

It is missional.

It is Christlike.

The Church of Clean Speech

Imagine a community where words are sacred.

Where:

- "Yes" means yes—without follow-up texts, explanations, or guilt.
- "No" means no—without fear of rejection or offense.
- Promises are kept.
- Agreements are honored.
- Speech is not hurried, not excessive, not artificial.

This is what Jesus is forming.

Not just holy hearts—but holy mouths.

Because if we cannot speak truth, we cannot preach it.

And if we cannot be trusted in small words, we cannot be entrusted with the Word.

Let the Mountain Speak

This is not about rigid speech.

It's about radiant integrity.

Jesus is crafting a people who don't rely on verbal gymnastics to convince others.

They don't inflate their words.

They don't manipulate with tone or volume.

They don't weaponize flattery.

They speak with clarity.

They love with truth.

They walk in the light—and so their speech reflects the Light.

A Heart Anchored in Yes

Let your yes be yes.

Let it echo the steadiness of your Savior.

Let your no be no.

Let it come from the strength of your boundaries, not the fear of others.

And let every word in between be filtered through the Spirit of Truth who lives inside you.

The mountain still speaks.

And this time, it calls not for an oath, but for a voice that needs no oath at all.

Chapter III
Turning the Other Cheek — The Fire of Mercy

> *"Ye have heard that it hath been said, An eye for an eye, and a tooth for a tooth: But I say unto you, That ye resist not evil: but whosoever shall smite thee on thy right cheek, turn to him the other also."*
>
> —*Matthew 5:38–39, KJV*

This is the sound of Heaven undoing the law of retaliation.
Not by negating justice—but by revealing a higher justice: the justice of mercy.
The law had permitted proportionate response:
    If a man injured your eye, the law allowed the same in return.
    It was never meant to encourage revenge—only to limit it.
But Jesus now offers something radical:
    Don't strike back.
    Don't retaliate.
    Don't mirror the wound.
    Instead—turn the other cheek.

A Kingdom Without Retaliation

This command is not weakness.

It is not passivity.

It is not surrender to abuse.

It is the refusal to let evil shape your response.

Jesus is not telling us to ignore injustice.

He is commanding us to interrupt its cycle.

When someone slaps you, your flesh demands revenge.

But the Kingdom calls for fire—but of another kind:

> The fire of mercy that consumes hatred instead of fueling it.

To turn the other cheek is to say:

> "You cannot define me with your violence."

> "You will not make me hate."

> "I belong to a different Kingdom."

The Power of Holy Resistance

Turning the cheek is not weakness.

It is strength under control.

It is the choice to overcome evil not by copying it,

but by confronting it with an unbreakable spirit.

Jesus Himself lived this command:

- When mocked, He was silent.
- When struck, He did not return the blow.
- When crucified, He forgave.

This was not submission to injustice.

It was the conquest of it.

He did not lose—He loved.

He did not shrink—He shined.

Practical Mercy in a Violent World

Jesus expands this call even further:

> "And if any man will sue thee at the law, and take away thy coat, let him have thy cloak also."

> "And whosoever shall compel thee to go a mile, go with him twain."

These are not calls to martyrdom.

They are invitations to generosity in the face of oppression.

- Don't just meet expectations—exceed them with grace.
- Don't just obey the law—fulfill it in love.
- Don't just endure the injustice—transform it by your response.

This is the upside-down ethic of the Kingdom:

> You don't fight like the world fights.

> You love until hate has no ground left to stand on.

A New Kind of Fire

This is not natural.

The natural man wants vengeance.

But the spiritual man is filled with a new kind of fire.

A fire that burns not to destroy, but to refine.

A fire that turns the other cheek, not because it hurts less—but because it matters more.

To turn the other cheek is not to ignore pain,

but to testify that Christ is worth more than revenge.

It is to absorb the blow with eternal purpose.

To hold your ground with holy gentleness.

To reveal the cross-shaped love that defeats darkness.

The Mountain Still Speaks

These are not easy words.

But they are Jesus' words.

He did not come to make you comfortable.

He came to make you like Him.

And He is the One who bore the beating, carried the cross, and still looked on His enemies and said,

"Father, forgive them…"

That is the fire of mercy.

So, when you're struck—turn.

When you're sued—give.

When you're forced—walk further.

Not because you're weak—but because your strength is resurrection strength.

The mountain still speaks.

And it says,

"Do not repay evil for evil. Overcome evil with good."

Chapter IV
Love Your Enemies
— The Perfection of the Father

"Ye have heard that it hath been said, Thou shalt love thy neighbour, and hate thine enemy. But I say unto you, love your enemies, bless them that curse you, do good to them that hate you, and pray for them which despitefully use you, and persecute you; That ye may be the children of your Father which is in heaven..."

—Matthew 5:43–45, KJV

This is the summit.

The most staggering command ever spoken.

The final stroke of Jesus' brush painting the true portrait of a child of God.

Love your enemies.

Not tolerate them.

Not politely ignore them.

Love them.

The Radical Reversal

The old teaching had twisted Scripture.

"Love your neighbor" was God's Word—

But "hate your enemy" was man's addition.

Jesus exposes the counterfeit and reveals the true standard of Heaven.

Enemies are not outside the reach of your love—

They are the proving ground of it.

"But I say unto you…"

That phrase again.

It cuts like a blade through human instinct and pride.

Jesus isn't giving you a new suggestion.

He's delivering the DNA of Heaven.

What It Looks Like

He breaks it down with divine clarity:

1. Bless those who curse you.

    Speak well of those who mock and insult you.

2. Do good to those who hate you.

    Not just avoid them—serve them.

3. Pray for those who use and persecute you.

    Not bitter prayers, but sincere intercession.

This isn't normal.

It isn't cultural.

It's supernatural.

And that's the point—

This kind of love does not come from you.

It comes from the Father.

The Signature of Sonship

"That ye may be the children of your Father…"

How does the world know you are His?

Not by your theology alone.

Not by your miracles.

Not even by your church attendance.

But by this:

> *"He maketh his sun to rise on the evil and on the good, and sendeth rain on the just and on the unjust." (v. 45)*

The Father is not selective with His mercy.

He pours it out freely—even on those who defy Him.

And you—child of God—must do the same.

Beyond Human Love

"If ye love them which love you, what reward have ye?"

That's not divine.

That's human.

Even sinners, Jesus says, love their friends.

But Kingdom people are marked by a higher love.

A love that doesn't flinch at betrayal.

A love that keeps giving, even when it's rejected.

This love does not originate in the emotions—

It flows from the Spirit.

You cannot fake it.

You cannot manufacture it.

You must receive it from God to release it to your enemies.

Perfect as the Father

> *"Be ye therefore perfect, even as your Father which is in heaven is perfect." (v. 48)*

The word perfect here is teleios—meaning complete, mature, whole.

It does not mean flawless performance.

It means perfected love.

Love that has grown beyond conditions.

Love that reflects the Father's fullness.

You are not called to be perfect in performance—

You are called to be perfect in love.

That is the goal.

That is the identity.

That is the image of Christ within you.

The Mountain Still Speaks

Enemies will come.

Curses will be spoken.

Hate will rise.

Persecution will press.

But the voice of the Mountain still speaks—calling you to respond with the impossible:

- To bless.
- To serve.
- To pray.
- To love.

This is not idealism.

It is the invitation to sonship.

To forgive like Jesus.

To shine like your Father.

To walk in a love that cannot be shaken.

Chapter V
The Secret Life
— Giving Without Applause

"Take heed that ye do not your alms before men, to be seen of them: otherwise ye have no reward of your Father which is in heaven. Therefore, when thou doest thine alms, do not sound a trumpet before thee, as the hypocrites do... that they may have glory of men. Verily I say unto you, they have their reward. But when thou doest alms, let not thy left hand know what thy right hand doeth..."

—Matthew 6:1–3, KJV

Some treasures are hidden in vaults.
Others are stored in secret places of the heart.
But Jesus says there is a treasure greater than all.

The reward of the Father
Given not to the loud, but to the hidden.
Not to the applauded, but to the unseen.

The Religion of Applause

The religious elite had mastered visibility.

They gave offerings with public display—sometimes literally sounding trumpets in the temple courts.

Their generosity was theatrical.

And it worked—

People clapped.

People praised.

But Heaven was silent.

   "They have their reward…"

They were seen by men—

But not by God.

When the Right Hand Doesn't Know

Jesus flips the script.

He tells His followers to give with such humility that even their left hand doesn't know what their right hand is doing.

It's a poetic way of saying:

   Let your giving be so private, so natural, so sincere, that you yourself forget to keep track.

   No bragging.

   No posting.

   No inner scoreboard.

   Just pure compassion, flowing freely—no strings, no spotlight.

The Father Sees in Secret

   "And thy Father which seeth in secret himself shall reward thee openly."

This is not about being anti-public.

It's about being anti-performance.

Jesus is not condemning all visible acts of kindness—

He's condemning the motivation to be seen.

When you give in secret:
- You place your confidence in the Father's eyes, not man's.
- You trust that He is not blind.
- You let go of the need to be celebrated.

And in time—He will reward you.

Maybe not with riches.

But with something greater:

His approval, His intimacy, His likeness.

The Purity Test of the Kingdom

Giving is a test.

Not of wealth—

But of heart.

Do you give to be praised?

Or do you give because love compels you?

This is the test of the secret life—the part of you no one else sees.

The part only God measures.

The Kingdom is built not just on great acts—but on pure motives.

Don't Trade Glory for Likes

We live in an age where even charity has a camera angle.

But Jesus warns:

> If you give for man's glory, you've already been paid.
>
> You don't need to announce everything.
>
> You don't need the public's claps.
>
> You don't need the Instagram caption.
>
> You need the Father.
>
> And He sees in secret.
>
> And what He sees, He rewards.

The Mountain Still Speaks

The Kingdom does not run-on performance.

It runs on purity.

Not purity of image—

But of intent.

So, give.

Give generously.

Give privately.

Give until your left hand forgets.

Because in that moment,

Heaven remembers.

And the mountain still speaks—

From the quiet place,

The humble place,

The secret place.

Chapter VI
When You Pray
— Enter the Secret Place

> *"But thou, when thou prayest, enter into thy closet, and when thou hast shut thy door, pray to thy Father which is in secret; and thy Father which seeth in secret shall reward thee openly."*
>
> —Matthew 6:6, KJV

There is a door few ever open.

A narrow door.

A quiet door.

It is not found in cathedrals or beneath stained glass.

It does not swing with public spectacle or spiritual noise.

It is the entrance to a hidden realm—where only the soul and God meet.

It is the narrow gate of prayer.

And it requires something the world does not value:

Silence. Surrender. Secrecy.

The Stage vs. the Secret

Jesus begins not by teaching technique, but by exposing motive.

"And when thou prayest, thou shalt not be as the hypocrites are…"

They loved public stages.

Standing in synagogues.

Shouting in streets.

Performing in the name of God but not speaking to Him.

Prayer became theater.

The heart was absent.

God was not their audience—people were.

Jesus disarms it all with one command:

"Go into your room. Shut the door."

The Closet: A Sacred Chamber

In Hebrew tradition, the idea of the "secret place" echoed the Holy of Holies — that inner sanctuary where only the high priest entered.

Now, Jesus tells every believer:

You have access.

You are welcome.

You are invited.

Not just to speak, but to dwell in the presence of the Father.

To "shut the door" means to leave behind:

- Applause
- Distraction
- Pretense
- Comparison
- Noise

It is a gate so narrow, only you and God can fit through.

The Posture of the Narrow Gate

The narrow gate is not defined by difficulty—but by depth.

It's not about trying harder—

It's about surrendering deeper.

True prayer begins when:
- You stop trying to impress God
- You let go of needing to impress others
- You speak from your true voice, not your polished one
- You don't just talk—you listen

The secret place teaches you:
- To be still
- To wait
- To ache
- To hunger
- To trust

There is no room for performance here.

Only presence.

What the Father Sees

"Your Father who sees in secret…"

This is not a distant deity.

This is a God who watches the moments no one else notices:
- When your tears fall in prayer.
- When your heart breaks in silence.
- When your lips whisper names too sacred to post.
- When you lay your fears on the floor before Him.

He sees.

And what He sees in secret, He rewards openly.

Not always in riches—but in something better:

Peace. Identity. Power. Joy. Holiness.

The Narrow Way Is the Only Way

The narrow gate of prayer is not optional.

It is the only path into the heart of the Father.

You cannot fake intimacy with God.

You cannot substitute noise for nearness.

There is no shortcut.

There is no public entrance.
The world shouts.
But the Kingdom whispers.
The Father doesn't dwell in your performance—he waits in your silence.

How Few Enter
Many speak of God.
Few speak to Him.
Many pray with volume.
Few pray with honesty.
Many repeat words.
Few commune.
The secret place is narrow because it costs something:
- Your pride
- Your time
- Your convenience
- Your ego
- Your distractions

But what you gain is everything.

The Mountain Still Speaks
Jesus did not teach prayer to the crowds first—he retreated to lonely places and modeled it.
He taught His disciples not just how to pray, but where and why.
He pointed not to temples, but to closets.
Not to repetition, but to relationship.
So, when you pray—shut the door.
Still your soul.
Speak simply.
Listen deeply.
The Father is there.
And the mountain still speaks—calling you not to say more, but to be with Him more.

Chapter VII
Hallowed Be Thy Name
— Unlocking the Lord's Prayer

"After this manner therefore pray ye: Our Father which art in heaven, Hallowed be thy name."
—Matthew 6:9, KJV

Jesus has just invited His disciples into the secret place.

Now, he hands them the language of Heaven.

Not a chant.

Not a formula.

But a pattern.

A blueprint.

The Lord's Prayer is not simply words to repeat—

It is a spiritual skeleton—holding the weight of all true communion with God.

And it begins here:

"Our Father… Hallowed be Thy Name."

Our Father

He is not a distant force.

He is not merely Creator or Judge or Master.

He is Father—

Near. Personal. Intimate.

But Jesus does not say, "My Father."

He says, "Our Father."

Prayer begins with belonging—with family, with unity, with shared grace.

We come to God not as strangers, but as sons and daughters, and we come together.

No one monopolizes God's ear.

No one stands alone in prayer.

The first word Jesus gives is "Our."

That's the Kingdom:

> Collective intimacy with a holy Father.

Which Art in Heaven

The Father is close, but He is also enthroned.

He is in Heaven—above politics, storms, injustice, and time.

He is not shaken by our chaos.

To say "which art in heaven" is to lift your eyes—to remember where your help comes from.

You are not praying to a god limited by earth.

You are praying to the King of all.

He sees the full picture.

He governs in wisdom.

He hears in power.

Hallowed Be Thy Name

Here lies the posture of true prayer:

Worship before request.

Adoration before petition.

"Hallowed" means holy, sacred, set apart, revered.
This is not just about using God's name reverently—
It's about living in a way that reveals His holiness.
When we pray, "Hallowed be Thy Name," we are asking:
> "Let Your name be made holy through my life."
> "Let my speech, actions, thoughts, and love reflect who You truly are."

This is a dangerous prayer.
Because it demands transformation.

Why This Order Matters

We often rush into prayer with:
- "God, help me."
- "God, fix this."
- "God, bless me."

But Jesus slows us down.
Before you ask for daily bread, before you confess your sins, before you plead for protection—stop and behold His holiness.
When the name of God is hallowed in your heart, everything else falls into place.

Hallowing His Name Today

To hallow God's name means:
- You don't take it in vain.
- You don't attach it to lies.
- You don't use it to manipulate.
- You lift it up with your life.

It means you live as if the whole world is watching how you reflect Him.
Because they are.
The name of God is not just to be worshiped on Sunday.
It's to be hallowed in your Monday speech, your Tuesday choices, your Wednesday trials.

When you forgive, you hallow His name.

When you stay pure, you hallow His name.

When you trust in the storm, you hallow His name.

The Mountain Still Speaks

The prayer Jesus gave us is the most repeated in history, but it is also the most ignored in spirit.

"Hallowed be Thy Name" is not the introduction—
It is the foundation.

Until the name of God is set apart in your heart, your prayer life will be small, shallow, and self-centered.

But when you begin here—with awe, wonder, trembling, and love—you enter into a depth few ever reach.

The mountain still speaks:

Come and see the Father.

Come and revere His name.

Come and make your life a living "Amen" to the holiness of God.

Chapter VIII
Thy Kingdom Come
— The Surrender of Sovereignty

"Thy kingdom come. Thy will be done in earth, as it is in heaven."
—*Matthew 6:10, KJV*

This is not a wish.
This is a summons.
It is a call for Heaven to take ground—in your life, in your city, in your world.
It is not praying for escape.
It is praying for invasion.
"Thy kingdom come" is not about leaving Earth—
It's about transforming it.

What Is the Kingdom?
The Kingdom of God is not a nation.
It is not a church building.
It is not political.

The Kingdom is the rule and reign of God—
Wherever His will is obeyed,
His presence is welcomed,
His name is hallowed,
That is where the Kingdom is.
And Jesus came not to fit into kingdoms—
But to establish His own.
To pray "Thy Kingdom come" means:
- "Take over, Lord."
- "Reign here."
- "Break the systems that oppress."
- "Dismantle the lies that bind."
- "Let Heaven rule."

A Dangerous Prayer

"Thy Kingdom come" is not just a safe, spiritual phrase.
It's a dangerous act of surrender.
Because before the Kingdom comes to the world—
It must come to you.
And that means:
- Dethroning your ego
- Laying down your control
- Submitting your ambitions
- Yielding your plans

You cannot pray "Thy Kingdom come"
if you're still building your own.

Thy Will Be Done

These words change everything.
They are not passive.
They are powerful submission.
You're not just saying,
  "Do what You want, God."

You're saying:

"Make my heart want what You want."

This is where the battle is won—in the hidden place of surrender.

Jesus Himself prayed these words in Gethsemane:

"Not my will, but thine, be done."

And through His surrender, redemption came to the world.

On Earth as It Is in Heaven

Heaven is not distant.

It is near.

And Jesus tells us to pray it here.

In Heaven:

- God's will is not debated.
- His presence is not resisted.
- His name is not profaned.

Now He says:

"Ask for that reality to come here."

This prayer reshapes how we live:

- We don't settle for spiritual apathy.
- We don't give up on justice.
- We don't accept sin as normal.
- We become ambassadors of Heaven.

What Does It Look Like?

When His Kingdom comes:

- The poor are honored.
- The proud are humbled.
- The sick are healed.
- The captives are freed.
- The lonely are loved.
- The Name of Jesus is lifted high.

You become a carrier of that Kingdom.

In your words.

In your decisions.

In your kindness.

In your suffering.

You don't just wait for Heaven.

You bring it with you.

The Mountain Still Speaks

The cry of the Kingdom is not:

"Bless what I'm doing, God."

But:

"Do what You desire, God—through me."

This is not a sideline faith.

This is the front lines.

To pray "Thy Kingdom come" is to say:

"I'm done with comfort.

I'm done with control.

I surrender to Your higher purpose."

It is the prayer of prophets.

The language of martyrs.

The heartbeat of Christ Himself.

And still, the mountain speaks:

"The Kingdom is at hand.

Prepare the way.

Open the gates.

Yield to the King."

Chapter IX
Daily Bread
— Trusting God for Today

"Give us this day our daily bread."
—*Matthew 6:11, KJV*

After revering God's name…

After surrendering to His Kingdom and will…

Jesus teaches us to ask for something beautifully simple:

Bread.

Not luxury.

Not excess.

Not tomorrow's provision.

But today's sufficiency.

The Heart of the Prayer

This line may seem ordinary.

But it is deeply spiritual.

It teaches us to:
- Acknowledge God as our Provider
- Live in the present
- Depend on His faithfulness day by day

Jesus didn't tell us to pray for monthly supplies or long-term security. He said:

"This day... our daily bread."

Just like the manna in the wilderness,

He gives enough for today.

And tomorrow?

We trust again.

Bread as a Symbol

"Bread" is more than food.

It represents:
- Sustenance for the body
- Strength for the soul
- Everything essential for life and purpose

To pray for daily bread is to say:

"Father, give me what I need to live, love, and obey today."

Not what I think I need.

Not what the world says I need.

But what You know I need.

The Spirit Behind the Ask

Notice:

It's not "Give me my daily bread."

It's "Give us our daily bread."

Even in provision, Jesus calls us to remember:

We are not alone.

This prayer holds no greed.

It is the language of community.

To pray this rightly is to ask not only for yourself, but for the widow, the orphan, the neighbor, the friend, the stranger.

It is a reminder:

> "If I have more than I need, maybe I am someone else's answer to this prayer."

What It Isn't

This prayer is not:
- A license for laziness
- An excuse not to plan
- A call to reject work

But it is a call to trust:
- In seasons of lack
- In times of fear
- In days of uncertainty

To pray this daily is to resist anxiety.

To say:

> "I will not worry about tomorrow.
>
> I will trust You with today."

A Rebuke to Self-Sufficiency

In the West, we stock pantries and insure futures.

But often we forget the Source.

"Daily bread" reminds us:

> We are not our own providers.
>
> No amount of wealth changes our dependence on God.

Jesus Himself, in the wilderness, defeated the enemy's temptation with this:

> *"Man shall not live by bread alone, but by every word that proceedeth out of the mouth of God." (Matthew 4:4)*

So yes—pray for physical bread.

But never forget the Word is your deeper sustenance.

The Mountain Still Speaks

The world says:

- Secure more.
- Hoard more.
- Worry more.

Jesus says:

"Trust Me.

Today.

Again.

And again tomorrow."

This prayer is the rhythm of Heaven.

A daily inhale of faith.

A daily exhale of fear.

Every time you pray:

"Give us this day our daily bread," you silence the lie of scarcity and awaken the truth of divine sufficiency.

Still the mountain speaks:

"You are not forgotten.

You are not forsaken.

He who fed the five thousand still sees you.

And His bread never runs out."

Chapter X
Forgive Us
— The Link Between Mercy and Freedom

"And forgive us our debts, as we forgive our debtors."
—Matthew 6:12, KJV

In the sacred rhythm of prayer, after daily bread comes the next essential need:

Mercy.

We do not live by food alone.

We live by the forgiveness of God and the forgiveness we extend to others.

This line is not a polite request.

It is the cry of the soul:

"I am in debt… and I cannot pay."

The Word "Debts"

Jesus doesn't use the word "sins" here—He says debts.
Because sin isn't just rebellion—
It's a spiritual obligation unpaid.
A weight we owe, but cannot settle.
A burden we carry, but cannot lift.
To ask for forgiveness is to admit:

> "I am morally bankrupt before You.
> My good deeds are not enough.
> Only grace can cancel my account."

The Condition

> "As we forgive our debtors…"

This is the only line in the Lord's Prayer with a condition built in.
Jesus is saying:

> "Don't just ask for forgiveness—extend it."

God's forgiveness is not a pond that we hoard—
It's a river meant to flow.
To be forgiven, and yet refuse to forgive, is to block the flow of Heaven.
It is spiritual hypocrisy—asking God to do for us what we withhold from others.

Mercy Reveals Sonship

Forgiveness is not weakness.
It is the strength of the Kingdom.
When you forgive:

- You break cycles of revenge
- You release others from judgment
- You free yourself from bitterness
- You mirror the heart of God

Jesus, hanging on the cross, prayed:

> "Father, forgive them…"

He had every right to withhold mercy—but He gave it anyway.

To walk in unforgiveness is to walk away from the cross.

What Forgiveness Is (and Isn't)

Forgiveness is:

- Letting go of the right to retaliate
- Trusting God to be Judge
- A choice before it's a feeling
- A command, not a suggestion

Forgiveness is not:

- Ignoring injustice
- Pretending pain never happened
- Reconciliation without repentance

You can forgive someone, even if relationship is not restored.

Because forgiveness sets you free, not just them.

Why We Struggle

Forgiveness feels impossible when:

- The wound is deep
- The offense is repeated
- The pain is still fresh

But here's the Kingdom key:

> You don't forgive from your strength—
>
> You forgive from the mercy you've received.
>
> If He has erased your debt, can you not release theirs?
>
> Forgive Us… Again and Again

This prayer reminds us:

> Forgiveness is not a one-time event.
>
> It is a daily posture.
>
> Because sin is not rare.
>
> And mercy must be constant.
>
> Every day you breathe, you need the oxygen of grace.
>
> Every time your heart beats, you are living on undeserved kindness.

So, keep the flow open.

Don't block it with resentment.

Don't poison it with pride.

Let mercy move.

The Mountain Still Speaks

Still He speaks, from the heights of the mountain:

"Let go.

You were forgiven much.

Forgive much."

Let that bitter root be pulled.

Let that weight be lifted.

This is the scandal of the Kingdom:

You are released, when you release others.

You are freed, when you set others free.

And every time you say,

"Forgive us our debts, as we forgive…" you echo the mercy of Christ and the voice of the mountain.

Chapter XI
Lead Us Not Into Temptation — The Prayer for Guidance and Strength

"And lead us not into temptation, but deliver us from evil."
—Matthew 6:13, KJV

This is the most misunderstood line in the Lord's Prayer.

Would God ever lead us into temptation?

The answer is no—for God *"tempteth no man" (James 1:13)*.

Yet Jesus still commands us to pray:

"Lead us not into temptation."

This is a plea for guidance, for strength, and for protection.

It's a cry from a soul that knows its own weakness and dares not walk a single step without God's hand.

The Journey of the Soul

We walk through a world filled with snares.

- Snares of pride
- Snares of lust
- Snares of greed
- Snares of despair
- Snares hidden in plain sight

Temptation is not just a moment of seduction—

It is a pathway that leads you away from the will of God.

To pray this line is to say:

> "Lord, keep my feet from that path.
>
> Place warnings in my spirit.
>
> Guard my mind before I wander."

What Temptation Really Means

Temptation (Greek: peirasmos) can also mean:

- A trial
- A test
- A proving ground

Some tests come from God, like Abraham's or Job's.

But temptation, as a pull toward sin, comes from the enemy.

We do not pray to avoid all trials—

We pray for the strength to overcome.

This line is not a request to live a pain-free life.

It is a humble cry for divine leadership—for the Lord to guide us through, and if possible, around the snares that destroy.

Deliver Us from Evil

The Greek can also read:

> "Deliver us from the evil one."

We are not just asking for general protection.

We are acknowledging there is an adversary.

Satan is real.

Temptation is real.

And we are not strong enough on our own.

The one who prays this understands:

> "I am vulnerable.
>
> But I am not alone."

This is not fear—

This is wisdom.

When You're in the Middle of the Temptation

Sometimes the prayer comes too late to avoid temptation.

You're already in it.

Already wrestling.

Already weak.

This prayer is still for you.

> "Deliver me, Lord.
>
> I stepped too close.
>
> I wandered in.
>
> But You are my escape."

God doesn't just prevent temptation.

He provides a way out *(1 Corinthians 10:13)*.

Even if you fall—

This prayer pulls you up.

Even if you wander—

This prayer brings you home.

The War You Cannot See

There is a spiritual battle raging over your soul.

And this prayer is part of your armor.

- Every time you ask for guidance, you sharpen discernment.
- Every time you cry for deliverance, angels are dispatched.
- Every time you recognize your weakness, He becomes your strength.

Temptation may whisper...

But the Spirit shouts back, "Not today."

The Mountain Still Speaks

Still the voice of Jesus echoes from the summit:

> *"Watch and pray, that ye enter not into temptation." (Matthew 26:41)*

This is not a passive religion.

This is an active dependence.

To follow Christ is to walk through a world on fire with your eyes on the Shepherd and your feet on His path.

So pray it every day:

> "Lead me, Lord.

Away from the trap.

Away from the lie.

Away from the cliff's edge.

And when I am close—deliver me."

The mountain still speaks:

> The path is narrow, but His hand is strong.

Chapter XII
For Thine Is the Kingdom
— Living in the Power of the Amen

"For thine is the kingdom, and the power, and the glory, forever. Amen."
—Matthew 6:13b, KJV

The final line is not a whisper.

It is a roar.

It is the thunderous "Amen" that shakes both Heaven and earth.

It is the bold declaration that God reigns—not just in theory, not just in history, but right now, forever, without rival.

This is how Jesus taught us to end our prayers:

In worship.

In victory.

In assurance.

Why This Ending Matters

The Lord's Prayer begins with "Our Father"—and it ends with His Kingdom, His power, His glory.

In between are our needs:

- Daily bread
- Forgiveness
- Guidance
- Deliverance

But the beginning and the end are all about God.

This is no accident.

It's a holy pattern:

Start with His holiness.

End with His greatness.

Live every line in between under His rule.

Thine Is the Kingdom

It's not mine.

Not Rome's.

Not Babylon's.

Not America's.

Not the devil's.

The Kingdom belongs to God.

This means:

- The rule is His
- The agenda is His
- The timeline is His
- The final word is His

To say, "Thine is the Kingdom," is to let go of control and rejoice that the real King is still on the throne.

And the Power

We are weak.

He is not.

Our prayers are not effective because we speak them—but because His power backs them.

The Greek word used here is dynamis—the same root for dynamite.

That's what's behind your whispered prayer.

That's what fuels your daily "Amen."

He is able:

- To save
- To heal
- To restore
- To raise the dead
- To bring justice
- To crush darkness

Thine is the power.

And the Glory

All of it—

The beauty, the majesty, the wonder, the awe—

It belongs to Him.

We do not pray to build our name, but to magnify His.

We live, not to impress the world, but to reflect the glory of the Father.

This is why we forgive.

This is why we endure.

This is why we pray:

That He would be glorified.

When the world sees us live out this prayer, they should say:

"Surely, God is with them."

Forever

Not for a season.

Not until the world falls apart.

Not just while life is good.

Forever.

The Kingdom does not expire.

The power does not weaken.

The glory does not fade.

The Amen of Heaven is eternal.

This is your anchor.

When kingdoms collapse, when strength runs out, when the world forgets—

He still reigns.

Amen

"Amen" means:
- "So be it"
- "It is done"
- "I agree with all of Heaven"
- "I stake my life on this truth"

It is not the end of the prayer.

It is the beginning of faith.

When you say "Amen," you're not closing a conversation—you're opening your life to everything you just prayed.

The Mountain Still Speaks

Still He speaks from the mountain:

"This is how you pray.

Not with fear.

Not with ritual.

But with reverence, surrender, trust, and power."

The final words lift your eyes.

They raise your soul.

They steady your feet.

You do not pray into the void.

You pray into a Kingdom unshakable.

So end with power.

End with certainty.

End with glory.

Say it loud:

> "Thine is the Kingdom,
>
> and the power,
>
> and the glory,
>
> forever.
>
> Amen."

Conclusion

The Echo That Never Fades

The mountain has spoken—

And still it speaks.

Not with thunder or fire.

Not with political decree or cultural noise.

But with the words of the King—spoken in stillness, etched in eternity, alive in every surrendered heart.

From "You have heard, but I say…" to "Thine is the Kingdom…" every line of this Sermon reveals not just a new way of life— but a new kind of human.

The Higher Ground

Jesus didn't invite His disciples to a palace.

He brought them up a mountain.

Not to intimidate—but to elevate.

To see the world from a Kingdom vantage point.

To hear Heaven speak above the madness of men.

To shape a people, not with violence, but with truth.

If you've made it to this final page, then you've heard what the world is still missing:

- That purity is power.
- That meekness is strength.
- That mercy wins.
- That secret sacrifice is seen by God.
- That the narrow way leads to life.

You Are the Echo Now

The mountain was not the destination.

It was the launch point.

The sermon was not just instruction.

It was impartation.

And now, you are the echo.

- In your patience, the Beatitudes are heard again.
- In your honesty, the truth still shines.
- In your generosity, the Father is revealed.
- In your quiet obedience, the world still hears the voice of Jesus.

Still He Speaks

Every time you forgive, the mountain speaks.

Every time you pray, the mountain speaks.

Every time you say no to temptation, and yes to the narrow way, the voice of the Rabbi echoes into a deaf world.

The Sermon is not finished.

It continues—in your steps, in your story, in your surrender.

You are not just a reader of this Word.

You are the living letter *(2 Corinthians 3:2)*.

So now, go back down the mountain.

Not unchanged.

Not unaffected.

But marked.

Filled.

Transformed.

And wherever your feet go—let the world say:

"Still He speaks."

Acknowledgments

To write about the words of Jesus is to step on holy ground.
To do so twice is to kneel in awe.
This book could not have come to life without the presence, prayers, and patience of those who walk with me on this Kingdom path.

To Feebe, my beloved wife and closest companion—
Your quiet strength, fierce love, and unwavering support are the voice of grace in my life.
Thank you for believing in the voice of the mountain, and in the voice He placed within me.

To my family, blood and spirit—
You've helped carry my fire, my burden, and my call.
This journey is richer because you walk beside me.

To the readers and seekers around the world—
You are why I write.
Every message, every testimony, every soul stirred by His Word reminds me that this isn't just a book.
It's a holy echo finding its way into modern hearts.

To the mentors, pastors, and teachers who first introduced me to the Sermon on the Mount—
Your voices still live in mine.

To those who pray in secret, fast without notice, forgive without reward—
This book was written with you in mind.
You are living the Sermon.
You are proving the Kingdom is real.

And finally, to the Lord Himself—the Voice from the mountain, the Word made flesh, the One who still speaks:

"This is all for You. Let Your Kingdom come."

— D.B.C.

About the Author

Damiano B. Centola is a writer, poet, and visionary thinker whose works explore the sacred intersection of theology, beauty, and truth. With a gift for transforming scripture into living language, he speaks not only to the intellect but to the soul.

His writings are marked by a deep reverence for the Word of God, a prophetic urgency for this generation, and an unwavering commitment to spiritual authenticity. Whether unpacking ancient texts or crafting new devotions, Damiano writes with fire, tenderness, and clarity.

He is the author of thirteen previous books, including:
- The Mountain Still Speaks Volume I Salt, Light, and Fire from the Sermon That Changed the World".
- The Mother of Corruption: Unveiling Spiritual Corruption from Babylon to Today.
- God's Sovereignty: Exploring the Divine Rule Over Creation, History, and Eternity.
- Divine Encounter: Discovering the Depth and Power of God's Names.
- The Lord Is My Shepherd: A Journey Through Psalm 23 — Meditations on Trust, Hope, and Eternal Love.
- I Choose the Call: My Daily Anthem of Devotion — A Journey of Faith, Purpose, and Obedience.

- The Mystery of Mysteries: Decoding the Divine Proportions of the Human Body Through Art, Anatomy, and Sacred Geometry.
- Jewish Holidays: Jesus Teaches Us Through Sacred Seasons.
- The Words of Jesus: Unlocking the Lord's Prayer in Aramaic, Greek, and English.
- YESHUA (ישוע): The Nazarene, the Refugee, the Redeemer.
- Yeshua the Builder: From Bethlehem to the Baptism.
- The Bread of Life: A Journey to Bethlehem.
- Water Jar: Devotions from the Shadows of Scripture.

Damiano's work is rooted in deep study, lived experience, and a passion for awakening hearts to the voice of Christ. He writes not to impress—but to invite the reader to higher ground.

He lives between continents, cultures, and callings, alongside his beloved wife, Feebe, whose song and spirit accompany every step of his journey.

Back Cover Blurb

Still He Speaks. Still the Mountain Echoes.

In a world chasing noise, success, and surface truths, the voice of Jesus still calls from the mountain—clear, radical, and unshakable.

In this bold and Spirit-led sequel to The Mountain Still Speaks, author Damiano B. Centola returns to the Sermon on the Mount to unpack the second half of Christ's most powerful message. From "You have heard, but I say…" to "Thine is the Kingdom," each chapter dives deep into the narrow way, the hidden life, and the fire of mercy.

This is not just a devotional.
It's a discipleship journey.

Here, the words of Jesus confront our comfort, awaken our spirits, and commission us to live as Kingdom people—uncompromising in love, truth, and surrender.

You'll never hear the Sermon the same way again.
Because it was never just spoken—
It was meant to be lived.

www.ingramcontent.com/pod-product-compliance
Lightning Source LLC
Chambersburg PA
CBHW061224070526
44584CB00029B/3983